NIGHT SKY WATCHER

Quarto is the authority on a wide range of topics.

Quarto educates, entertains and enriches the lives of
our readers—enthusiasts and lovers of hands-on living.

www.quartoknows.com

**Words in bold are explained
in the glossary on page 114**

To Kamini, Vikas and Sachin
– RP

Project Editor: Tasha Percy
Editorial Director: Victoria Garrard
Art Director: Laura Roberts-Jensen

For cobalt id
Editor: Marek Walisiewicz
Designers: Darren Bland, Rebecca Johns and Paul
Reid

Published in hardback in the United States by
QEB Publishing, Inc.
6 Orchard, Lake Forest, CA 92630

A CIP record for this book is available from the
Library of Congress.

ISBN: 978 1 60992 954 1

Printed in China

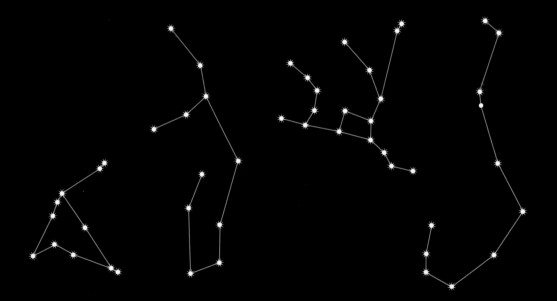

NIGHT SKY WATCHER

RAMAN PRINJA

QEB

Contents

Get to grips with the motion of the planets and understand why the stars and constellations seem to move from one night to the next.

Find out what equipment you need to watch the night sky comfortably and safely.

Binoculars will help, but you don't need them to explore the night sky.

Night Sky Essentials

Discover why some stars appear bright or colored, while others are dim.

Learn the differences between stars, planets, galaxies, and other objects in the sky.

What can you see?

On a clear night the sky is decorated with a fantastic display of objects. You may be able to see **stars** of different colors, bright **planets**, and a stunning **Moon**. Sometimes you'll be lucky enough to see a rare event such as a **meteor** shower, a **comet**, or an **eclipse**.

STAR OR PLANET?

The planets will usually be much brighter than most of the stars in the same area of the sky. The planets also don't twinkle as much as the stars. If you follow a planet over many nights, you should see that its position in the sky at the same time each night changes when compared to the stars.

Did you know?

Stars seem to twinkle in the night sky. This isn't because they get brighter and fainter, but because the air above us moves around and distorts their light before it reaches our eyes.

SPOTTING OBJECTS

The best thing about night sky watching is that everyone can do it. All you need are your eyes or some simple binoculars, and this book.

The Sun ▲

ASTROFACTS

>> Our nearest star is the Sun, which is 93 **million** miles away.

>> The next closest star to us is called Proxima Centauri. It is 25 **trillion** miles away—that's 25 with 12 zeros on the end!

◄ Mercury

LIGHTS IN THE SKY

Nearly all the tiny lights you see in the night sky are stars. Sometimes a planet may be in view. Mercury, Venus, Mars, Saturn, and Jupiter are the only planets that can be seen with an unaided eye. On a very dark and clear night, you may be able to see another galaxy—a vast but very distant collection of **billions** of stars.

Stars, planets, and galaxies

When you look up at the night sky, most of the twinkling lights you see are stars. So what are stars, and what makes them different from planets, **galaxies**, and other objects in the sky?

WHAT ARE STARS?

Stars are giant balls of gas. Most of the gas is **hydrogen**—the simplest of all the **elements**. The gas is squeezed together so tightly, and gets so hot, that it triggers a process called **nuclear fusion**. This releases huge amounts of energy, including the light that we can see from trillions of miles away.

WHAT ARE PLANETS?

When stars form, the edges of the **dust** clouds around them can clump together to form planets. Some planets are rocky, while others are made of gases or liquids. Jupiter, for example, is made mainly of hydrogen and **helium** gas.

Jupiter ▲

WHAT ARE GALAXIES?

Galaxies are enormous collections of stars, dust, and gas held together by gravity. Some contain trillions of stars and a few can be seen with the naked eye as faint smudges. Our Sun is part of a galaxy called the **Milky Way**.

▼ M101, the Pinwheel Galaxy

Did you know?

There are eight planets, including Earth, that go around our Sun. They formed about 4.5 billion years ago. New planets are still forming today around other stars.

Mercury ►

Venus ►

Earth ►

Mars ►

Star watching

If your eyesight is very good, and it's a really clear night, you should be able to see more than 2,000 individual stars—if you have the patience to count them! Take a closer look and you'll see that they're not all the same: they differ in brightness and color.

BRIGHT AND DIM STARS

Stars can appear bright because they are large and give out lots of light, or because they are closer to Earth than other stars. The brightest star in the night sky is called Sirius A, or the Dog Star. Another star, Rigel, is much bigger than Sirius A and gives out more light. But Sirius A looks brighter because it is 100 times closer to us.

◀ Sirius A

Rigel ▶

▼ Supernova

Imagine this

A supernova can release more energy in a few days than our Sun will give out over its whole life. You need to be very lucky to witness a supernova explosion— in our galaxy this event can be seen once every few hundred years.

THE LIFE OF STARS

Stars are born inside giant clouds of dust and gas called **nebulae**. The dust and gas clump together, growing into dense, hot masses. Once these grow big enough, nuclear fusion begins and the star starts to shine. Stars also die as they use up their hydrogen fuel. Some shrink away, while others explode violently into **supernovae** and form **black holes**.

▲ Sharpless 2-106 nebula

COLORFUL STARS

Stars appear as tiny spots of light, but they don't all have the same color. There are red, blue, and yellow stars. Their colors are different because some stars are cooler (the red ones) and others are much hotter (blue ones).

Did you know?

All the stars you can see with your naked eye are part of our galaxy—the Milky Way. There are more than 200 billion stars in the Milky Way and about 100 billion other galaxies in the universe.

▲ Nebulae are giant star factories and look amazing through powerful **telescopes.**

Patterns in the sky

With so many objects in the night sky, how do you find your way around? How can you tell which star is which? The answer is to look for the patterns made by the stars. These patterns stay the same from one night to the next, making them great signposts in the sky.

Pleiades ▼

STAR CLUSTERS

Some star patterns exist because their stars are close to each other and were born around the same time. You can see some of these **star clusters**, such as the Pleiades (or Seven Sisters), with your naked eye. They look even better through binoculars.

IMAGINED PATTERNS

Most of the star patterns you can see in the sky are imagined. The shapes—such as animals or objects—result from the chance alignment of stars that are not related in any way and may in fact be hundreds of **light-years** apart. These patterns are called **constellations**.

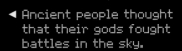

◄ Ancient people thought that their gods fought battles in the sky.

THINGS TO DO

It's fun to look at a star-filled sky and invent your own constellation. First, make a small picture frame from cardboard—about 4 by 4 inches. Hold the frame at arm's length and look through it, moving around the sky until you find a group of bright stars that fall within it. Try to imagine a shape by "drawing" lines between five or seven stars in the frame. You could picture an animal or an object. What would you call your new constellation? See if you can find your constellation a few nights later.

Did you know?

Most of the constellations were made up a long time ago by ancient Greek and Arab explorers. The constellations were named after the shapes of animals, gods, or other figures in their myths and stories.

▲ The Big Dipper

The constellations

With a little practice, you'll soon learn how to recognize the shapes and patterns in the sky, known as constellations. Spotting well-known constellations will help you get your bearings and move between objects in the sky.

YOUR GUIDES TO THE SKY

There are 88 constellations used today to map out the sky. If you live north of the **equator**, you can see about 60 constellations; if you are in Earth's Southern **Hemisphere**, you can see about 30. Some can be seen from almost anywhere in the world. This picture shows the shapes of just a few of the constellations you might see in the night sky.

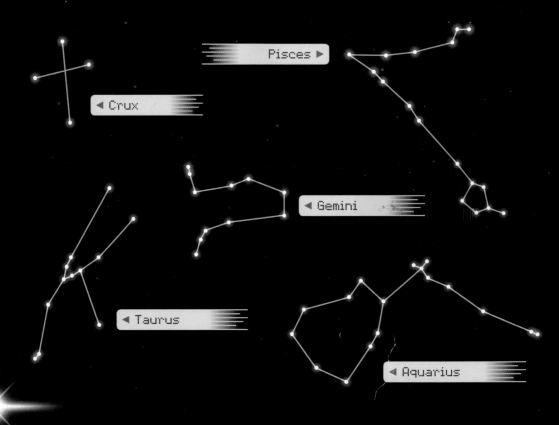

Pisces ▶

◀ Crux

◀ Gemini

◀ Taurus

◀ Aquarius

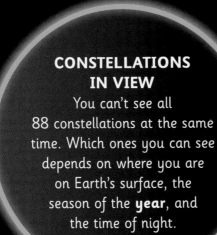

CONSTELLATIONS IN VIEW

You can't see all 88 constellations at the same time. Which ones you can see depends on where you are on Earth's surface, the season of the **year**, and the time of night.

LOOKALIKE?

Some of the constellations do look like the thing they are named after. The constellation Leo (the Latin word for "Lion"), for example, does resemble a lion. But does the pair of stars in the constellation Canes Venatici ("The Hunting Dogs") really look like a pair of dogs?

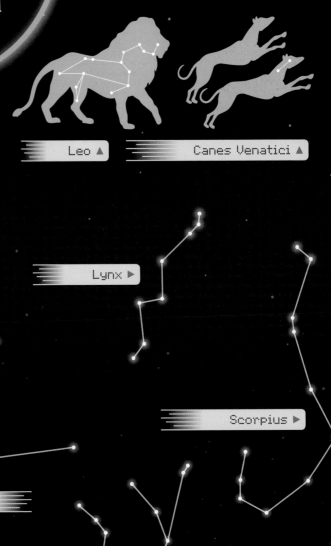

Leo ▲

Canes Venatici ▲

Virgo ►

Lynx ►

▲ Aquila

Scorpius ►

◄ Carina

Ursa Major ►

Stars seem to move ▶
around in the sky.

The moving sky

Once you can recognize the shape of a few constellations, pick one and try following it over a few hours. Check its position once every 30 minutes or so and you should notice that it seems to move across the sky. But it's not the sky that's moving—it's our planet, Earth.

SPINNING EARTH

Imagine a giant rod that passes through Earth, from the North **Pole** to the South Pole. Just like a spinning top, Earth spins on this rod (or axis). It makes one full turn every day. As Earth turns, some parts receive the light of the Sun, while others are dark. That's what gives us night and **day**. As Earth turns, the stars in the night sky—just like the Sun in the daytime sky—seem to move slowly.

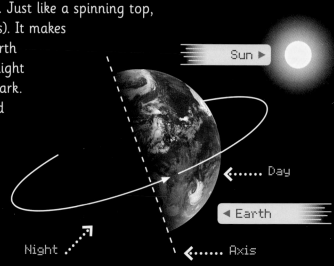

Sun ▶

◀······ Day

◀ Earth

Night ·····⫶

◀······ Axis

STAR TRAILS

If you watch the stars for a few hours, you'll see that they seem to rotate around one point in the sky. This is the top of the imaginary rod that passes through Earth's poles. You can see how they rotate in a photograph that was taken over a few hours.

CONSTANT SHAPES

Even though the stars seem to move across the sky, the patterns of the constellations stay the same. The spacing you see between groups of stars doesn't change. A constellation may rise, move above you, turn sideways or even upside down, but it won't spread apart or change shape.

Did you know?

In the Northern Hemisphere, the top of the imaginary rod passing through Earth's poles points toward a star called Polaris. This is also called the North Star because it always shows which way is north.

5pm ►

8pm ►

11pm ►

◄ How the constellation Cassiopeia seems to move over one night.

2am ►

◄ 5am

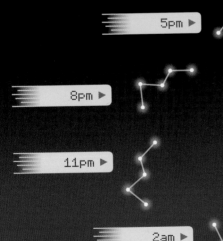

Our changing view

Not only do the stars seem to move during the course of one night, but they also seem to shift from one month to the next. This is because Earth **orbits** the Sun, bringing different constellations into view at different times of year.

A YEAR IN ORBIT

Our planet takes one year to complete a single **orbit** of the Sun. We can see stars only at night, because they are too faint to spot during daylight. As Earth moves around the Sun, the stars we can see at night change very slowly from one day to the next. You'll notice the change if you look up at the same part of the sky at the same time of night every month.

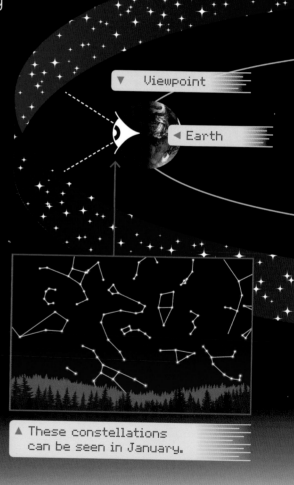

▼ Viewpoint

◄ Earth

▼ In 1530, the Polish scientist Nicolaus Copernicus was the first to argue that the Earth orbited the Sun.

▲ These constellations can be seen in January.

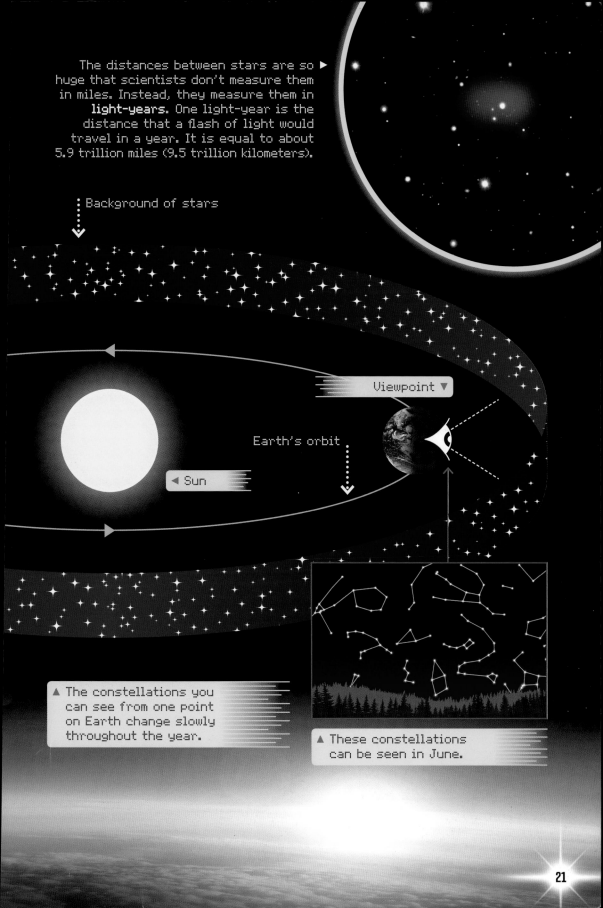

The distances between stars are so ▶
huge that scientists don't measure them
in miles. Instead, they measure them in
light-years. One light-year is the
distance that a flash of light would
travel in a year. It is equal to about
5.9 trillion miles (9.5 trillion kilometers).

Background of stars

Viewpoint ▼

Earth's orbit

◀ Sun

▲ The constellations you
can see from one point
on Earth change slowly
throughout the year.

▲ These constellations
can be seen in June.

Finding your way

The stars seem to move in the night sky in complicated ways. So how can you find your way around? The easiest way is to look for star patterns, or constellations, and use them to point the way to other objects in the sky. You can also use a simple tool called a **planisphere**.

GET YOUR BEARINGS

In this book, you'll read that a star can be seen in the north or in the west. So you'll need a simple compass to know which way you are facing. The needle of the compass always points north.

STAR-HOPPING

Some of the constellations have very clear shapes and are easy to spot in the sky—especially when you have learned to recognize their outlines. Once you've found these "easy" constellations, you can draw imaginary lines between their stars. Following these lines will guide you to other nearby constellations, stars, and even galaxies. This is called star-hopping, and you can start doing it on page 28.

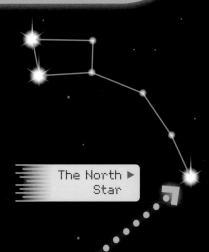

The North ► Star

◄ The Big Dipper

Imaginary line

▲ Extending an imaginary line from the two stars in the Big Dipper will point your way to The North Star.

MEASURING DISTANCE

If you need to describe how far one star appears to be from another, try using your hand! Looking at the sky, stretch out your arm as far as it will go. The width of your hand—or finger—is a quick and convenient measure of the relative distance between stars in the night sky.

PLANISPHERE

Latitude 40° North

NORTH

Eastern Horizon

Western Horizon

SEPTEMBER
OCTOBER
NOVEMBER
DECEMBER
JANUARY

3 AM
2 AM
1 AM
MIDNIGHT
11 PM
10 PM
9 PM
8 PM
7 PM
6 PM
5 PM
4 PM
3 PM
2 PM
1 PM
NOON
11 AM

4 AM
5 AM
6 AM

MAY
APRIL

DRACO
CEPHEUS
CASSIOPEIA
PERSEUS
TRIANGULUM
TAURUS
ORION
CETUS
ERIDANUS
FORNAX
ERIDANUS
LEPUS

Eastern Horizon

Ecliptic

Equator

► Set the date and time on the scale on the edge of the planisphere

USING A PLANISPHERE

A planisphere is a simple way of seeing which constellations are in view on a particular day and time. It is made of a circular plastic disc with an oval window cut into it. Underneath the plastic is a map of the stars and constellations. Turning the plastic disc to set the time and date will reveal the visible sky within the window.

Getting ready

Choosing the right time and place to watch the night sky will make all the difference to how much you see. Pick a clear night so that clouds don't block your view—and get ready with some simple equipment.

WHERE TO WATCH

Find a safe, dark place close to home. Backyards are great, but only if they are well away from streetlights or the lights of your house, which will spoil your view. Try a local park or playground, but always make sure you are supervised by an adult.

SPOTTING STARS

Wait about 10 minutes to let your eyes get used to the darkness—you'll see a lot more stars.

STAY WARM AND COMFORTABLE

Don't forget to wear warm clothes and a hat. Even spring and summer nights can become chilly. You'll be staring at the sky most of the time, so get comfortable. Lying back on a deck chair or a waterproof groundsheet will let you look up without straining your neck.

▼ Moonless nights are best for stargazing—that's because the bright light reflected from the Moon makes it harder to see fainter stars and planets.

Did you know ?

Your eyes are more sensitive to faint light when you don't look directly at an object. So when you're struggling to see a distant star, look just slightly to one side of it.

THINGS TO DO

Take a small flashlight and stretch some red plastic wrap over its light. Keep the plastic in place with a rubber band. Using this red light outside will let you read this book and see where you're going without spoiling your night vision.

Seeing more

Using just your eyes, you'll be able to see stars, trace the shapes of the constellations in the sky, spot meteors, and follow the movements of five planets. But add a pair of binoculars and you'll be able to see faint stars, look at details on the Moon's surface, and even make out the moons of the planet Jupiter.

BINOCULARS

You may already have a pair of binoculars at home. They're great for watching the night sky because they're light and always ready for action. If you're planning on asking for a pair as a present, look for ones marked 7 x 50 or 10 x 50. The first number gives their magnification and the second number tells you the **diameter** of the main lens in millimeters. The wider this lens, the more light it can gather to make faint stars seem brighter.

THINGS TO DO

Why not hold a star party? Invite your friends and family over on a dark, clear night and use your know-how to guide them through the wonders of the Moon, stars, and planets!

THINGS TO DO

The best way to learn the patterns of stars in the night sky is to draw them using a pencil and paper. First, choose an area of the sky. Draw large dots for the brightest stars in that area, then fill in fainter stars as smaller dots. Make notes about what you see—some stars have a red or blue color, for example.

Red star

Bright blue star

KEEP STEADY

When you use binoculars, the stars may appear to wobble. That's because binoculars magnify any movement of your hands. Try resting the binoculars on a fence or bracing them on your knees to keep them steady.

Find your way around the night sky using familiar pointer stars.

Explore the constellations and trace out shapes of monsters and heroes in the sky.

Spot distant stars, galaxies, giant dust clouds, and other exotic objects by "hopping" around the constellations.

Star-Hopping

Get to know the names of the stars and constellations.

Learn how to find the North Star and you'll never get lost again!

Orion

Orion ("The Hunter") is one of the easiest patterns to identify in the sky. Two of the ten brightest stars seen at night are in this constellation.

BETELGEUSE
This star is a red **supergiant**, more than 650 times the size of the Sun.

MAIN STARS
Orion is made up of seven main stars called Betelgeuse, Rigel, Bellatrix, Saiph, Alnitak, Alnilam, and Mintaka.

ORION'S BELT
Alnitak, Alnilam, and Mintaka make up the belt of Orion the Hunter.

RIGEL
This star is a rare blue supergiant that shines 100,000 times more powerfully than the Sun.

SPOTTING ORION

If you live in the Northern Hemisphere, Orion is easy to find in winter. Face southeast and look up halfway between the horizon and overhead. You should spot three bright stars close together in an almost straight line. These make up Orion's Belt. Head upward from the belt and you'll come to a bright, reddish star called Betelgeuse, which marks the shoulder of the Hunter. Head down and south from the belt stars to a bright blue star, Rigel. It marks Orion's left foot.

◄ Orion's shape was imagined to be a hunter holding a club in one hand and a shield in the other.

▼ Orion Nebula

Did you know?

A huge star-making factory called the Orion Nebula is located just below Orion's Belt.

Star-hopping
to Canis Major

Once you've found Orion, you can use it as a signpost to find the nearby constellation of Canis Major ("The Great Dog"). This includes the brightest star in the night sky—Sirius—as well as five other very bright stars that make its doglike shape.

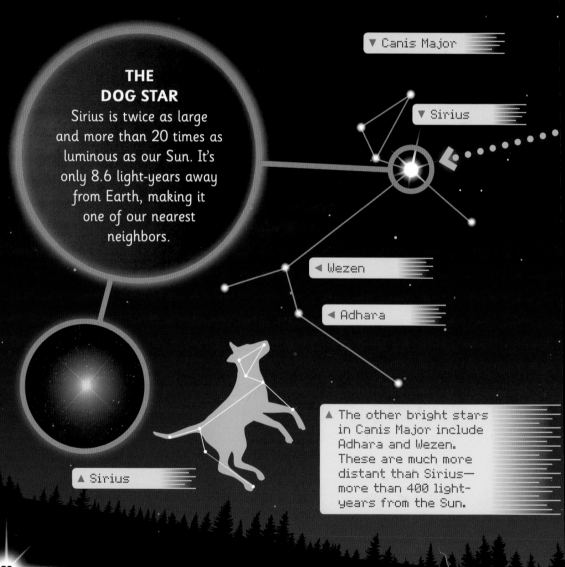

▼ Canis Major

THE DOG STAR

Sirius is twice as large and more than 20 times as luminous as our Sun. It's only 8.6 light-years away from Earth, making it one of our nearest neighbors.

▼ Sirius

◄ Wezen

◄ Adhara

▲ Sirius

▲ The other bright stars in Canis Major include Adhara and Wezen. These are much more distant than Sirius—more than 400 light-years from the Sun.

Sirius was known to the ancient Egyptians as the Nile Star. When it could be seen in the morning before sunrise, it was a sign that the great Nile River was about to flood.

▲ Orion

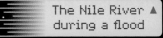

The Nile River ▲ during a flood

HOPPING TO CANIS MAJOR

Find the three stars of Orion's Belt. Now draw an imaginary line through the belt and down toward the horizon. Follow this line and you will easily spot a very bright star called Sirius. Sirius is in the constellation of Canis Major ("The Great Dog"), and Sirius itself is sometimes called the dog star!

Star-hopping
to Taurus and the Pleiades

Using Orion's Belt as a pointer in the sky, it is easy to find the constellation of Taurus ("The Bull"). Nearby, look for a beautiful jewel-like cluster of stars

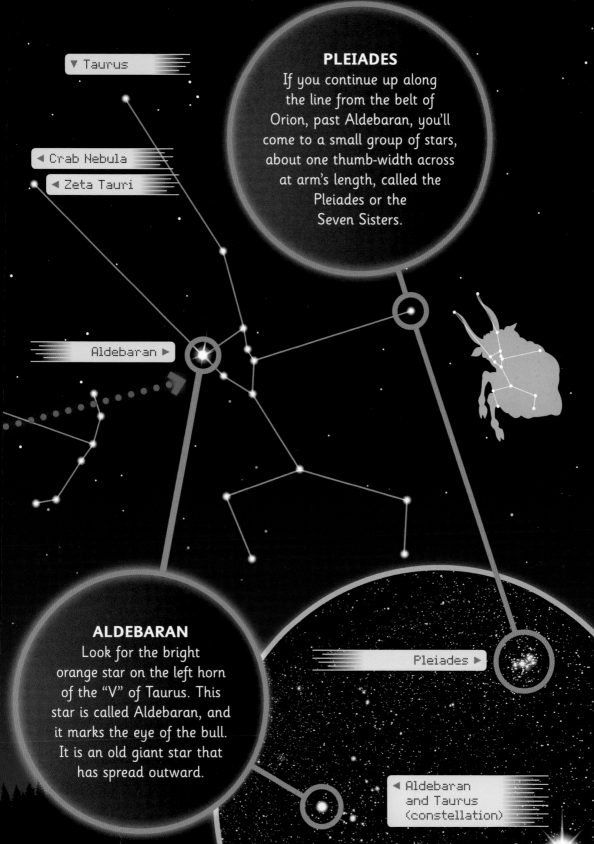

▼ Taurus

◄ Crab Nebula

◄ Zeta Tauri

PLEIADES
If you continue up along
the line from the belt of
Orion, past Aldebaran, you'll
come to a small group of stars,
about one thumb-width across
at arm's length, called the
Pleiades or the
Seven Sisters.

Aldebaran ►

ALDEBARAN
Look for the bright
orange star on the left horn
of the "V" of Taurus. This
star is called Aldebaran, and
it marks the eye of the bull.
It is an old giant star that
has spread outward.

Pleiades ►

◄ Aldebaran
and Taurus
(constellation)

The Big Dipper

High in the sky in spring and summer, you can see one of the most famous of all star patterns—"The Big Dipper." This grouping of seven stars is actually the brightest part of a bigger constellation called Ursa Major ("The Great Bear").

▲ Alkaid

Megrez ▲

HANDLE
The stars that make up the "handle" of the Big Dipper are Alkaid, Mizar, and Alioth.

Phecda ▶

SPOTTING THE BIG DIPPER

The Big Dipper is visible all year round in the Northern Hemisphere. This constellation is made up of seven bright stars that form the shape of a ladle or a saucepan with a long handle. In the middle of summer, you can easily see it in the northern part of the night sky. To find it, first look for the "handle" and then pick out the stars that make up the "bowl." Holding your hand out at arm's length, the Big Dipper is about two full hands across.

◀ Powerful telescopes have shown that Bode's Galaxy has a **spiral** shape, like our galaxy, the Milky Way.

SPOTTING BODE'S GALAXY

It's hard to see other galaxies with your naked eye. But with a pair of binoculars, you should be able to spot Bode's Galaxy. It looks like a blurry patch over the Great Bear's shoulders.

▼ Dubhe

◀ Merak

ASTROFACTS

>> The stars in the Big Dipper are about 75 to 125 light-years away from Earth.

>> The Big Dipper has other names in different countries. In India it's called "The Seven Sages," in England "The Plow," and in China "The Northern Ladle."

SAUCEPAN

The "bowl" of the Big Dipper is made up of four stars—Megrez, Phecda, Merak, and Dubhe.

Star-hopping
to Ursa Minor and the North Star

Knowing the stars of the Big Dipper will help you find the nearby constellation of Ursa Minor ("The Little Bear") and locate the North Star, or pole star. This star, also called Polaris, is directly over Earth's North Pole. So, if you face Polaris, you'll know that you're facing north.

▼ The Plough

◀ Ancient navigators used instruments like this quadrant to measure the position of the North Star and find their location, even when they were sailing the oceans far away from any landmarks.

Merak ▶

THINGS TO DO

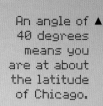

The North Star not only shows you which direction is north, but also tells you how far you are from Earth's equator. Stretch out both of your arms. Point one at the North Star and one at the horizon below it. The angle between your arms tells you your **latitude**. If you are at the equator, it will be zero (your arms will be together); if you are at the North Pole, it will be 90 degrees (a right angle).

An angle of ▲ 40 degrees means you are at about the latitude of Chicago.

Ursa Minor ▲

URSA MINOR

The North Star is part of the constellation called Ursa Minor. Its shape is a bit like that of the Big Dipper, but it is smaller and much fainter in the sky. See if you can make out its shape after you've found the North Star.

HOPPING TO THE NORTH STAR

Find the two stars—Dubhe and Merak—at the front of the "bowl" of the Big Dipper. Draw an imaginary line between them and upward. Move along this line about five times the distance between Dubhe and Merak and you'll arrive at the North Star, Polaris.

POLARIS

Other stars seem to move around in the sky, but Polaris stays fixed in the same position. This made it a great help to ancient navigators and explorers.

Star-hopping to Leo

The stars of the Big Dipper can be used to find the constellation of Leo ("The Lion"). Leo is one of the few constellations that really looks like what it is supposed to show, so look out for the lion in the night sky!

THE TERRIFYING LION

In Greek myth, Leo was a fearsome lion that terrorized the people of Nemea. Its skin was so tough that no one could kill it with a sword or spear. The lion was finally killed by the hero Hercules, who strangled it to death.

THE LEONIDS

Every November a shower of meteors called the Leonids seems to stream out from the region of the constellation Leo. The meteors burn up as they streak through Earth's **atmosphere**, producing a fantastic fireworks display overhead.

▼ The Big Dipper

◄ Megrez

HOPPING TO LEO

You can easily see Leo in spring in the Northern Hemisphere and in fall in the Southern Hemisphere. First find the stars Megrez and Phecda in the Big Dipper. Follow a line between these stars toward the horizon. You'll come to a bright blue-white star called Regulus, which is in the constellation Leo.

▼ Denebola

ALGIEBA

After Regulus, the second-brightest star in the constellation is Algieba. Scientists think that it is orbited by a huge planet at least twice the size of Jupiter.

▼ Algieba

◄ Leo

▲ Regulus

Look at the stars around ▲ Regulus. Notice that they make a shape like a backward question mark, with Regulus at the bottom of the question mark.

Cassiopeia

The constellation Cassiopeia ("The Queen") is near the North Star, so it is nearly always visible if you are in the Northern Hemisphere. Its five brightest stars also make a clear "W" shape in the sky, making it easy to spot.

◄ Segin

RUCHBAH
This star is made up of two stars that are very close to one another and about 100 light-years away from Earth.

► In ancient myth, Cassiopeia was the wife of King Cepheus of Ethiopia. She believed that she was even more beautiful than the goddesses.

Ruchbah ▲
(also called Ksora)

SPOTTING CASSIOPEIA

If you live in the Northern Hemisphere, look toward the northeast soon after sunset on a clear fall evening. You'll see five stars that make a wide "W" shape, about one hand span across. If you live in the Southern Hemisphere, Cassiopeia appears low in the north at nightfall. It can also make an "M" shape, depending on the time of night.

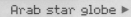
◄ Arab star globe ▶

Did you know?

The names of many stars, such as Segin and Ruchbah, come from ancient Arabic words. From the 10th to the 15th centuries, the Arab world was at the center of astronomical research.

SPINNING STAR

In the middle of Cassiopeia's "W" is Gamma Cassiopeia, a star that spins incredibly fast, throwing off material into the space around it. This makes it change in brightness throughout the year.

◄ Gamma Cassiopeia

Caph ▶

Shedir ▶

CAPH AND SHEDIR

These giant stars are about twice the size of the Sun.

Star-hopping to Perseus

Once you know the shape of Cassiopeia, you can use it to find the nearby constellation of Perseus ("The Hero"). Perseus follows Cassiopeia across the sky, night after night; it contains a couple of fantastic sights, so it is really worth exploring.

▼ Perseus holds a sword in one hand and Medusa's head in the other.

Mirphak ▼

◄ Mirphak is the brightest star in Perseus. This large star is more than 60 times the size of our Sun.

▲ Perseus

Medusa ▲

PERSEUS AND MEDUSA

Perseus is a character from Greek mythology who killed an ugly monster called Medusa. She had snakes for hair, and she could turn people to stone by looking at them.

Cassiopeia ▼

▲ Ruchbah

HOPPING TO PERSEUS

Perseus is quite a faint constellation, so it's best to look for it on a clear and moonless night, when Cassiopeia is high in the sky. Draw an imaginary line from the middle star of Cassiopeia's "W"— the star called Gamma Cassiopeia— above Ruchbah. Extend this line by about the width of Cassiopeia itself, and you'll reach an almost straight line of three stars, which make the arm and upper body of Perseus.

Imagine this

At least four of the stars in Perseus have planets going around them. Imagine what the surface and weather might be like on these planets. Could there even be strange life-forms thriving on them?

Star clusters ▼

CASSIOPEIA TO PERSEUS

On the way from Cassiopeia to Perseus, you'll pass a faint smudge. Look closely through a pair of binoculars and you may see that this is two star clusters, each containing hundreds of stars.

The Summer Triangle

The Summer Triangle is not really
a constellation but a pattern made
up of three stars in three different
constellations. The three stars—called
Vega, Deneb, and Altair—are all bright
and high up in the sky in the summer
months. Once you can find the stars,
you can use the triangle to explore
the night sky around them.

▲ Vega

◀ Deneb ▶

👓 SPOTTING THE SUMMER TRIANGLE

It takes a little practice to pick out this triangle in the sky. In
summer, face east in the late evening. Lie on your back and look up
for three especially bright stars high in the sky. Start with the blue-
white star Vega, almost directly above you. Then look down toward
the southern **horizon** to spot Altair, which is slightly less bright
than Vega. The distance from Altair to Vega is about two hand
spans. Then look northeast (to the left of Vega) to spot Deneb,
the third star in the triangle.

FINDING THE MILKY WAY

On a clear and moonless night, look between the stars Vega and Altair of the Summer Triangle. You may see a faint but broad band of light—this comes from the billions of stars in our own galaxy, the Milky Way. If you're lucky, you'll see a dark band across it. This is actually dust that blocks out the light in the background.

▼ Deneb

Vega ▼

◄ Altair

◄ Altair

ASTROFACTS

>> Deneb is a supergiant star that has almost 80,000 times the luminous power of the Sun. Deneb is faint because it lies almost 1,500 light-years from Earth.

>> Vega is 25 light-years away from Earth; about 1,000 years ago it was the North Star, like Polaris is today.

>> Altair is just 17 light-years from Earth; it is one of the closest stars you can see at night.

Star-hopping
to Cygnus, Lyra, and Aquila

This is a very simple star-hop. Once you can see the Summer Triangle, you've already found the three constellations Cygnus ("The Swan"), Lyra ("The Lyre", a type of musical instrument), and Aquila ("The Eagle").

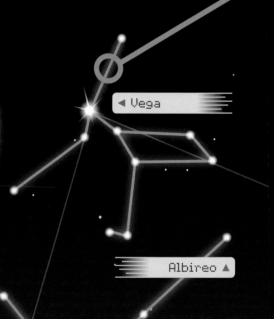

CYGNUS
Stretching its wings over the Milky Way, it's easy to see why this constellation is called the Swan. The tail of the swan is Deneb, one of the stars of the Summer Triangle, while its head is the star Albireo. This looks like a single star with the naked eye, but is actually two stars—a bright yellow one with a fainter blue partner.

◄ Vega

Albireo ▲

▲ Deneb

LYRA

The star Vega from the Summer Triangle is the brightest star in Lyra. It is the fifth-brightest star in the night sky. You can often see a parallelogram of four stars, which seems to be hanging from Vega.

Imagine this

The constellation of Cygnus is home to a black hole nearly 15 times the mass of the Sun. It spins 800 times a second and sucks in anything very close to it. Imagine what it would be like to fall into a black hole. You'd be stretched out like a piece of spaghetti!

▼ Tarazed

▲ Altair

AQUILA

Altair, the third star of the Summer Triangle, is the brightest star in this constellation, which looks like an eagle in flight. If you have a pair of binoculars, take a close look around the star called Tarazed. You should see a strange E-shaped area of darkness, almost as big as the full Moon. This is a giant cloud of dust that blocks out the light from the stars behind.

▼ The two brightest stars of the Summer Cross make up the long arm of the cross. They are called Acrux and Gacrux.

▼ Acrux

Gacrux ▲

The Southern Cross

If you live south of the equator, you'll nearly always be able to see the Southern Cross, or Crux, in the night sky. It is the smallest of all the 88 constellations, but is an important signpost to other stars. Ancient sailors used it to find their way around the seas.

SPOTTING THE SOUTHERN CROSS

The Southern Cross is in the night sky over much of the Southern Hemisphere, and rarely dips below the horizon. During midsummer, look toward the south and try to spot a cross or kitelike shape made up of four bright stars. This is the Southern Cross. It is very small—from top to bottom, it measures only the width of four of your fingers held up close together at arm's length.

▼ Coal Sack

◄ Right next to the Southern Cross, you may see a black patch on the background of the Milky Way. This is called the Coal Sack, and it is a giant cloud of dust called a dark nebula.

New Zealand flag ▼

◄ Milky Way

The Southern Cross ► is so famous that it even appears on the national flags of Australia and New Zealand.

CHECK OUT THE MILKY WAY

On a moonless night, away from bright city lights, look for a band of stars stretching across the sky from south to north and passing through the Southern Cross. This band is the Milky Way. It appears as a slightly lighter band of sky and is packed with a huge number of stars.

Star-hopping
to Centaurus

The Southern Cross is a great starting point from which to explore other constellations in the Southern Hemisphere. From here you can easily find Centaurus ("The Centaur")—one of the largest and most interesting constellations in the sky.

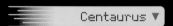

Centaurus ▼

The constellation of ▶ Centaurus almost wraps around the Southern Cross.

Omega ▲ Centauri

OLD FRIENDS

In the middle of the body of the Centaur is what looks like a smudged star. You can see it with your naked eye. This not a single star, but a cluster of more than one million stars called Omega Centauri. **Astronomers** think that it is more than 12 billion years old—one of the oldest things in our galaxy.

HOPPING TO CENTAURUS

Start at the Southern Cross. Draw an imaginary line between the two stars in the short arm of the cross. Move along this line from the darker star in the arm to the brighter one, then continue for three times this distance. You will arrive at a bright star called Beta Centauri. A little farther along the imaginary line, you'll come to Alpha Centauri, the brightest star in this constellation.

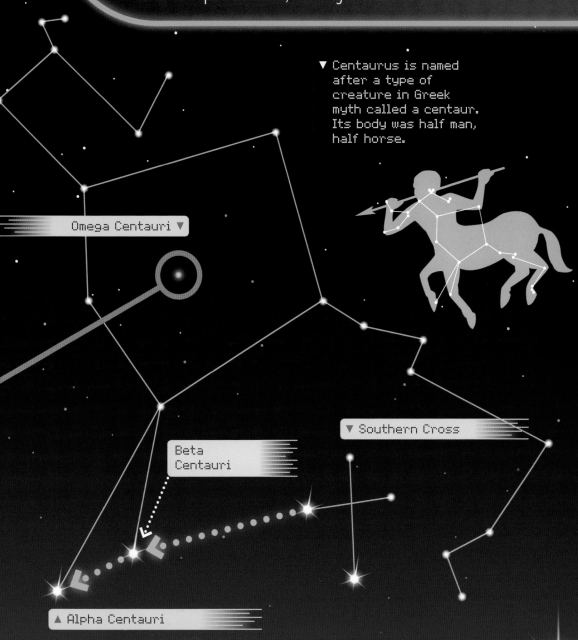

▼ Centaurus is named after a type of creature in Greek myth called a centaur. Its body was half man, half horse.

Omega Centauri ▼

▼ Southern Cross

Beta Centauri

▲ Alpha Centauri

Look for the phases of the inner planets, Mercury and Venus.

Find out what makes Mars the "Red Planet" and what Saturn's rings are made of.

Learn about the orbits of the planets and how this affects what we can see from Earth.

How did the planets form and what are they made of?

Discover the best times to spot the planets in the night sky.

The Planets

ASTROFACTS

>> The Sun and planets formed out of a giant cloud of gas and dust about 4.5 billion years ago.

>> Spacecraft have visited every planet in the solar system, and we have landed probes on the surfaces of Venus, Mars, Saturn's moon Titan, some comets, asteroids, and, of course, Earth's own Moon.

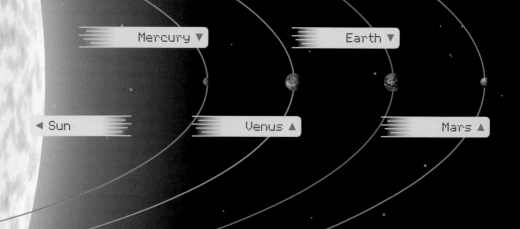

Mercury ▼

Earth ▼

◄ Sun

Venus ▲

Mars ▲

The solar system

With the Sun at its center, our **solar system** has eight planets—including Earth—as well as more than 150 moons. Smaller objects such as **asteroids** and comets are also part of the solar system, which is all held together by the giant Sun's **gravity**.

ORBITING THE SUN

The **planets** and other objects in the solar system orbit around the Sun. Almost all follow a path roughly around the Sun's equator. They orbit at very different speeds. The closest planet to the Sun, Mercury, moves at nearly 106,000 miles per hour, while the farthest, Neptune, moves at 12,000 miles per hour.

▼ Jupiter

Uranus ▼

Neptune ▲

Saturn ▲

SEEING THE PLANETS

Planets shine by reflecting light from the Sun. They do not make their own light. The brightness of planets changes depending on how far away they are from the Sun and how much of the sunlit side is facing us. Venus and Jupiter can appear brighter than even the brightest stars, such as Sirius and Vega.

Planet watching

Five planets in our solar system are bright enough to be seen without binoculars or a telescope. These are the three rocky planets, Mercury, Venus, and Mars, and the two giant gas planets, Jupiter and Saturn. Large telescopes are required to get a good view of the other planets, Uranus and Neptune, because they are so far away.

THE PATH OF THE PLANETS

The planets move from east to west across the sky. They all follow roughly the same path as the Moon and Sun. This means that sometimes the planets appear to be close together in the sky, or even line up.

▼ Jupiter

Did you know ?

The planets all move at different speeds and take different times to complete an orbit around the Sun. Saturn takes 30 years, Mercury just 88 days. The result is that they don't appear in the same part of the sky from one year to the next.

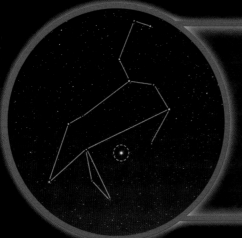

FINDING PLANETS

Because of their complex movements, the best way to find a planet in the sky is to check an astronomy magazine or website. This will tell you which constellation the planet passes through at any time of year. Find the constellation and look for an "extra" star—this will be the planet!

▲ Mars in Leo

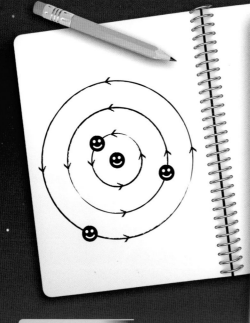

THINGS TO DO

Get together with a group of friends and try acting out how the planets move around the Sun. In a backyard or playground, mark out three large circles around the same center. Place one person at the center to be the Sun. Now three of you start walking around each of the three circles (orbits) to act as planets orbiting the Sun. Get the person in the inner circle to walk fastest and the person in the outer circle to walk slowest. Notice how the position of each person (or planet) changes compared to the others. That's why the movement of the planets, as seen from Earth, appears to be complicated.

▼ Mars

◀ Venus

◀ Saturn

▲ On some nights, you can see several planets at the same time.

Venus

Venus is often mistaken for a UFO because it is the brightest object in the sky after the Sun and Moon, and it seems to hover low over the horizon. On a dark, moonless night, the light from this planet can even cast a shadow here on Earth.

THE GREENHOUSE PLANET

Venus is almost the same size as Earth, but it orbits closer to the Sun than our planet does. Thick clouds cover Venus's surface and its atmosphere acts like a giant greenhouse, raising **temperatures** on Venus to around 890 degrees Fahrenheit. That's hot enough to melt lead!

◀ Like a greenhouse, the atmosphere of Venus traps heat from the Sun. A long time ago, Venus may have been much cooler.

MAKE A DATE

From the Northern Hemisphere, good times to see Venus are:
- summer 2015 in the evening
- fall 2015 before dawn
- spring 2016 before dawn
- spring 2017 in the evening
- fall 2018 in the evening
- spring 2019 before dawn
- fall 2020 before dawn

SPOTTING VENUS

It's not always possible to see Venus. Although it is bright, it is also low in the sky, so it is often blocked by trees or buildings. The best times to look for Venus is either just before sunrise in the eastern sky, or just after sunset in the west.

Venus ▶

Moon ▶

ASTROFACTS

>> Venus is about 67 million miles from the Sun and around 7,500 miles across.

>> The planet's atmosphere is mostly **carbon dioxide.**

>> Gravity on Venus is almost as strong as on Earth.

This picture of ▲ Venus was taken by a spacecraft called Pioneer in 1979.

The phases of Venus

The brightness and size of Venus seem to change over time. This is because its orbit brings it closer to us and also takes it farther away from us. As it moves around the Sun, Venus goes through **phases** when seen from Earth, just like the Moon does.

THE CHANGING FACE OF VENUS

Like the Moon, Venus changes from a full disk, to a half disk, to a crescent in the sky, and then back to a full disk. This cycle takes about 584 days. As Venus comes closer to Earth, it can be seen in the evening sky. As it starts to move away from Earth, it is visible in the morning sky.

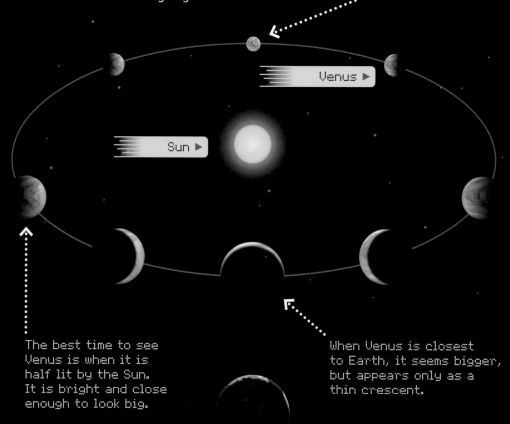

When Venus is on the other side of the Sun from Earth, it looks "full" but smaller.

Venus ▶

Sun ▶

The best time to see Venus is when it is half lit by the Sun. It is bright and close enough to look big.

When Venus is closest to Earth, it seems bigger, but appears only as a thin crescent.

Earth ▶

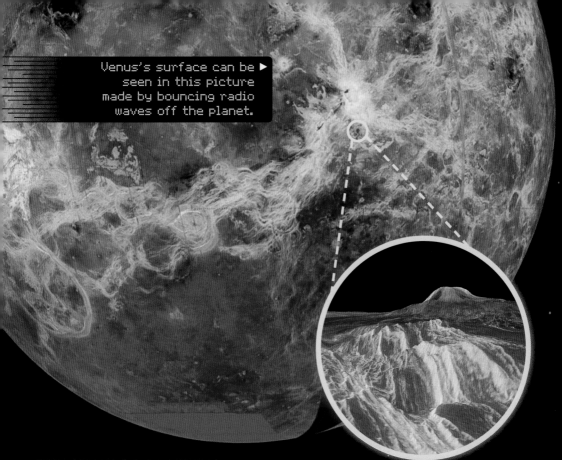

Venus's surface can be ▶
seen in this picture
made by bouncing radio
waves off the planet.

THE SURFACE OF VENUS

Although Venus is covered in thick clouds,
space probes have given us fantastic images of
its rocky surface. The planet has many of the
same features that we have on Earth—such as
volcanoes, mountains, plains, and craters.

▲ Valleys on Venus
can be up to 60
miles in length.

PROBING THE PLANET

Many spacecraft have been sent to Venus to probe
its atmosphere and surface. Some have even landed
on the planet. In 1982, a Soviet spacecraft called
Venera 13 was the first to send back color
photographs of the surface of Venus. The probe
lasted only a few hours on Venus's hot surface.

▲ Scientists assemble
the Venera 13 probe.

Mercury

Mercury is the closest planet to the Sun and takes just 88 days to complete a full orbit—which means that a year on Mercury is only 88 days long! Mercury is barely larger than our Moon, and even looks a lot like the Moon, with lots of craters on its surface.

SPOTTING MERCURY

Mercury is the smallest planet in the solar system and the closest to the Sun. It is difficult to spot because it is often hidden in the glare of the Sun. You can sometimes catch it as a bright morning or evening "star" about half an hour before sunrise or after sunset. You will never see Mercury in the middle of the night.

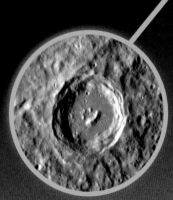

A crater on the surface ▶
of Mercury.

NORTH AND SOUTH

It's hard to wake up before dawn to see Mercury, so the best time to look is in the evening, just after sunset. If you live in the Northern Hemisphere, look for Mercury low in the sky toward the west after sunset between April and June. If you're in the Southern Hemisphere, try to spot it between September and November.

MISSION TO MERCURY

Since 2008, a NASA spacecraft called Messenger has been orbiting around Mercury, beaming back sharp images and data about the planet. Scientists are trying to understand more about how the planet formed and why it has water ice in its dark craters.

Mercury orbits closer to the Sun than the Earth. To see the tiny planet, you need to look toward the Sun after sunset or before sunrise.

▲ Special shields are used to protect Messenger from high temperatures so close to the Sun.

Jupiter ▼

▲ Mercury

Did you know ?

The planet Mercury was named after the Roman messenger god because it goes around the Sun so quickly. In the ancient myth, the messenger had both a winged hat and winged sandals to help him run swiftly.

◄ Roman God Mercury

Mercury's icy poles

Despite being close to the Sun, Mercury has ice in the craters near its poles. That's because sunlight never reaches into the depths of the craters, which remain at low temperatures.

▼ This picture, taken by NASA's Mariner 10 spacecraft, shows the scars on the planet's surface caused by impacts with asteroids.

PHASES OF MERCURY

Just like Venus and the Moon, Mercury has phases. It changes from full, to half, to a crescent, though you need a telescope to see these changes.

ASTROFACTS

>> Mercury is 36 million miles away from the Sun.

>> The planet is only slightly larger than Earth's Moon.

>> The temperature on Mercury's surface is around 850 degrees Fahrenheit during the day and -350 degrees or lower at night.

▼ Mercury orbits closer to the Sun than does our planet. Every few years it can be seen as a tiny black disk slowly moving in front of the Sun. This event is called a transit.

▲ A transit of Mercury across the Sun.

◄ Mercury's gravity is only about one-third as strong as Earth's—not strong enough to hold on to any atmosphere.

Mars

The planet Mars is our neighbor in space. It is often called the Red Planet because its surface is made up of rocks that are rich in iron oxide (rust). When seen with the naked eye, Mars looks like a bright star with a reddish color.

SPOTTING MARS

Mars is only half the diameter of Earth. Most of the time it looks like a reddish star in the sky. One way to tell it apart from stars is that Mars does not twinkle in the sky, while stars do.

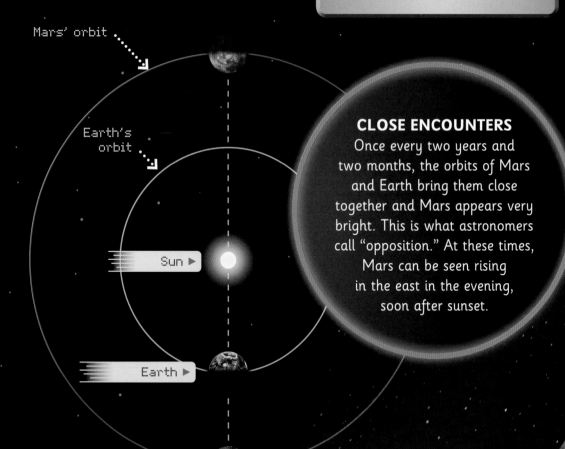

Mars' orbit

Earth's orbit

Sun ▶

Earth ▶

◀ Opposition

CLOSE ENCOUNTERS
Once every two years and two months, the orbits of Mars and Earth bring them close together and Mars appears very bright. This is what astronomers call "opposition." At these times, Mars can be seen rising in the east in the evening, soon after sunset.

Imagine this

Billions of years ago, there were rivers of water on the surface of Mars and maybe even an ocean. But the temperature on Mars became too low and its atmosphere too thin, and there is no liquid water there today.

LOOK FOR MARS AT ITS BRIGHTEST

Mars will be in opposition at these times. It will appear bright red and shine more than twice as brightly as the brightest star.
- April to June 2016
- July to September 2018
- October to December 2020

Mars, god ▶
of war

Mars seen ▶
in opposition.

THE GOD OF WAR

Mars is named after the Roman god of war, because of its blood-red color.

The Martian Surface

Mars is the only planet whose surface can be seen from Earth. With a good telescope you can see the bright ice caps on the planet's poles and a large dark area on its surface. But Mars also has vast extinct volcanoes and a huge canyon that splits the planet across the middle.

ASTROFACTS

>> Mars orbits at an average distance of 142 million miles from the Sun.

>> The planet is 4,222 miles across and its atmosphere is mostly carbon dioxide.

>> The temperature on Mars's surface is 28 degrees Fahrenheit in the daytime and −100 degrees or lower at night.

>> Mars has two small moons called Phobos and Deimos.

COULD I LIVE THERE?

Mars is a very unfriendly planet for humans. You wouldn't be able to breathe in the thin carbon dioxide atmosphere, and there is no liquid water on the surface today. A summer day on Mars might feel very pleasant and mild, but at night the temperature could drop below −100 degrees Fahrenheit.

Ice cap ▶

◀ A picture of
Mars taken by
the Mars
Surveyor
spacecraft.

Dark areas of dust ▶

Ice clouds ▶

Deep canyons ▶

MARTIAN "CANALS"

In the 19th century, astronomers looked at Mars through their telescopes and drew patterns they saw on its surface. They believed that Mars was crisscrossed by canals built by Martians. Using powerful telescopes and spacecraft, we've learned that the "canals" are channels carved by rivers that flowed there billions of years ago.

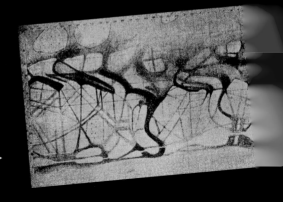

The "canals" on Mars, drawn by ▶
a 19th-century astronomer.

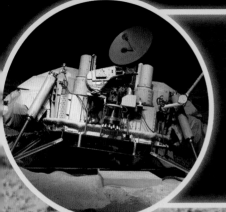

MISSIONS TO MARS

Mars has been explored by a series of spacecraft. The first probes landed on Mars in 1976. They were called Viking 1 and 2 and took amazing photos of the Red Planet. More recently, scientists have sent wheeled vehicles to Mars to explore its surface, monitor its dust storms and seasons, and test its soil for traces of life.

Jupiter

Jupiter is the largest planet in the solar system—so big that all the other planets could easily fit inside it. Jupiter appears white in the sky and shines brighter than the brightest star, Sirius, making it easy to spot.

SPOTTING JUPITER

Jupiter is so bright that it can even cast a faint shadow on a very dark night. It takes Jupiter almost 12 years to orbit the Sun. This means it moves slowly in our skies and can be visible in one constellation for many months. One of the best times to view Jupiter is when it is directly opposite the Sun, with Earth in between. At these times, Jupiter appears at its highest point in the sky around midnight wherever you live.

Earth ▶

Jupiter ▶

MAKE A DATE
To catch Jupiter at its brightest, look for it at the following times:
- February 2015 around the constellation of Cancer
- March 2016 around Leo
- April 2017 around Virgo
- May 2018 around Libra
- June 2019 around Ophiuchus

ASTROFACTS

>> Jupiter orbits the Sun at an average distance of 483 million miles.

>> The planet is 88,700 miles across.

>> The temperature at the tops of its clouds is -166 degrees Fahrenheit.

A GAS GIANT

Jupiter is a giant planet mostly made of hydrogen and helium gas, with no solid surface to stand on. It is surrounded by a very faint set of rings made of dark dust. There are at least 67 moons going around Jupiter, four of which are very large.

The giant planet

Jupiter's great size means that its gravity is two-and-a-half times as strong as it is on Earth. This big pull has trapped many moons and a system of dusty rings that now orbit the planet.

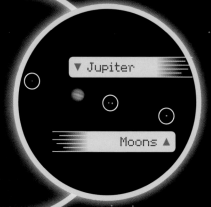

JUPITER'S MOONS

Try spotting Jupiter's moons. Look at the planet through a pair of good binoculars—you'll need to hold them very steady. You should notice up to four little dots in a straight line on either side of Jupiter. The dots are Jupiter's four largest moons, called Ganymede, Io, Europa, and Callisto. The moons orbit quickly around the giant planet. If you watch them over many nights, you will see that they change position around Jupiter.

▼ Jupiter

Moons ▲

Did you know?

Jupiter has a swirling atmosphere. A giant storm on Jupiter, called the Great Red Spot, has been blowing there for more than 300 years! This storm is so big that two Earths could fit inside it. The winds blow at speeds of more than 400 miles per hour.

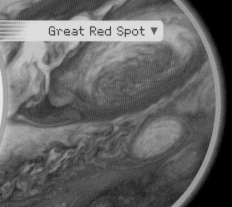

Great Red Spot ▼

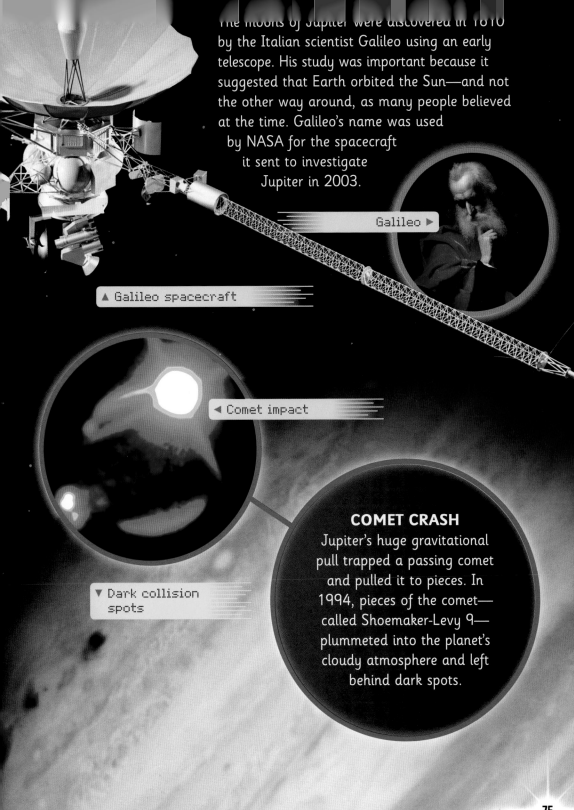

The moons of Jupiter were discovered in 1610 by the Italian scientist Galileo using an early telescope. His study was important because it suggested that Earth orbited the Sun—and not the other way around, as many people believed at the time. Galileo's name was used by NASA for the spacecraft it sent to investigate Jupiter in 2003.

Galileo ▶

▲ Galileo spacecraft

◀ Comet impact

▼ Dark collision spots

COMET CRASH

Jupiter's huge gravitational pull trapped a passing comet and pulled it to pieces. In 1994, pieces of the comet—called Shoemaker-Levy 9—plummeted into the planet's cloudy atmosphere and left behind dark spots.

Saturn

Saturn is the sixth planet from the Sun and the second-largest of the eight planets in the solar system. The distant planet appears pale yellow in the sky, always dimmer than Jupiter or Venus, but it still outshines almost all of the stars at night.

Inside Saturn's ▼ rings.

LORD OF THE RINGS

Like Jupiter, Saturn is a giant gas planet. Beneath clouds of hydrogen and helium gas, the interior gradually becomes a giant ball of liquid. Saturn is famous for the beautiful rings around its center, which are made of millions of rocks and lots of dust, all covered in ice.

Imagine this

Saturn is made mostly of hydrogen and helium, the lightest of all the chemical elements. So even though it is nearly ten times the diameter of our planet, its gravity is only a little stronger than Earth's.

SPOTTING SATURN

Saturn takes a long time to complete one orbit of the Sun—its year is more than 29 Earth years long! This means that Saturn appears to move very slowly across the background of constellations in the sky. It takes around two years to cross one constellation, which makes it fairly easy to see in the sky. It looks like a bright, golden star.

MAKE A DATE

To find Saturn, look for the constellation that it is passing through:

- From 2014 to 2015 Saturn will be in the constellation of Libra
- From 2016 to 2018 it will be in Ophiuchus

Saturn in Taurus ▲

Rings and moons

Saturn's amazing rings probably formed when asteroids and comets got too close to the planet and were torn apart by its gravity. The rings are around 150,000 miles across, but only a mile thick. Trying to spot the rings is a challenge, but it's worth a try for an exciting sight.

SPOTTING THE RINGS

You'll need a small telescope to see Saturn's rings. Choose a dark, clear night and look closely at Saturn; the rings will look like handles sticking out from either side of the planet.

Telescopic view ▲
of Saturn.

AT FULL TILT

When seen from Earth, Saturn's rings change their tilt toward us from year to year. Sometimes the rings are edge-on, and because they are very thin, we can't see them at all. From 2014 to 2020 the rings will be more "open" and facing us, making it a good time to look. The rings will be fully displayed in 2017, and Saturn will appear very bright.

◄ Saturn's rings tilt in and out of view every few years.

POLAR CYCLONES

NASA's Cassini spacecraft reached Saturn in 2004 and sent back some fantastic images of the planet. At the poles of the planet are huge cyclones—20 times as big as those on Earth. Heat from the interior of Saturn powers these giant thunderstorms.

▼ An artist's impression of Titan.

Did you know?

Saturn has 62 moons. The largest, called Titan, has an atmosphere. Scientists landed a spacecraft called Huygens on Titan in January 2005. The spacecraft sent back images to Earth showing that Titan is a strange place with lakes and rivers of oil!

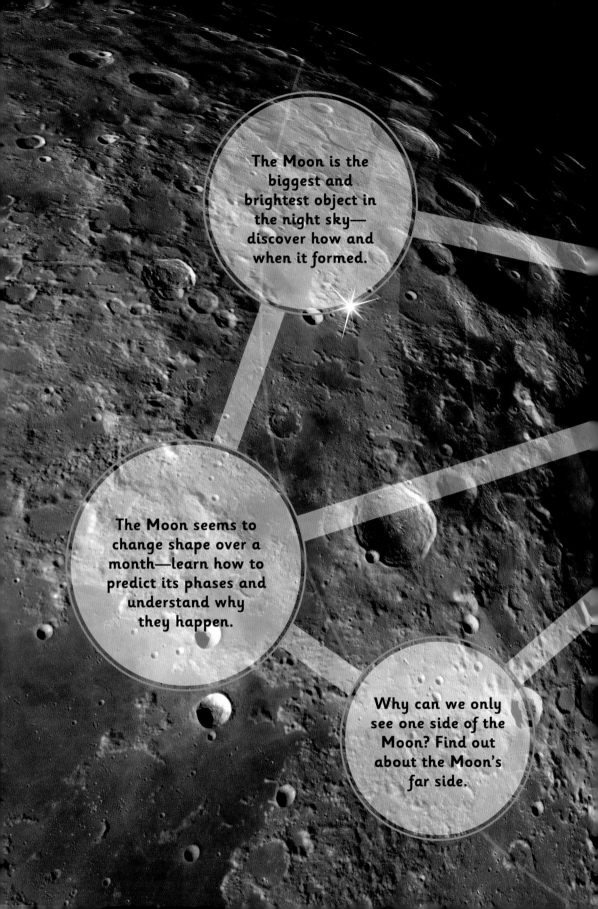

The Moon is the biggest and brightest object in the night sky—discover how and when it formed.

The Moon seems to change shape over a month—learn how to predict its phases and understand why they happen.

Why can we only see one side of the Moon? Find out about the Moon's far side.

The Moon

Observe the surface of the Moon and identify its craters and seas.

Find out where missions to the Moon have landed.

Moon watching

No matter where you live, the Moon is a wonderful object to explore at night. Unlike the stars, the Moon does not make its own light. The Moon shines because it reflects the light from the Sun. Since the Moon is much closer to us than the stars or planets, it is the brightest and biggest object in the night sky.

Did you know?

The Moon formed around 4.5 billion years ago when a rock as big as Mars smashed into Earth. Chunks of material broke off and went into orbit around our planet. Slowly, these rocks stuck together to become our Moon.

THE FAR SIDE OF THE MOON

From Earth, we can see only one side of the Moon. This is because the Moon spins at the same rate as it orbits the Earth, constantly turning one face away from us. The far side, sometimes called the "dark side of the Moon," can only be seen from a spacecraft.

SPOTTING THE MOON

When the Moon is in the sky, you won't have any trouble spotting it with your naked eye. Even a small pair of binoculars will reveal lots of detail on its surface.

ASTROFACTS

>> The Moon is about 236,000 miles away from Earth.

>> If Earth were the size of a basketball, the Moon would be the size of a tennis ball.

>> The Moon has no atmosphere. The temperature on its surface can drop to -238 degrees Fahrenheit.

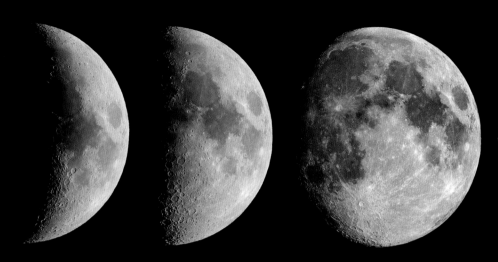

▲ Crescent Moon   ▲ Half Moon   ▲ Three-quarter Moon

The Moon's phases

We know that the Moon is ball-shaped, so why does it sometimes look like a circle and sometimes a crescent? Of course, the Moon itself doesn't change shape; what changes is how much of the sunlit part of the Moon we can see as it orbits Earth. The different shapes of the Moon are called its phases.

The date on which Easter ▶ Sunday falls is set by the phases of the Moon.

Did you know?

The phases of the Moon are very important to life on Earth. The tides in the Earth's seas, the behavior of animals, and even the dates of religious festivals are affected by the position of the Moon.

▼ Full Moon

Three-quarter Moon ▲   Half Moon ▲   Crescent Moon ▲

OUR VIEW OF THE MOON

From Earth, the phases of the Moon can be seen clearly. When the Moon is getting bigger in the sky, it is called a waxing Moon; when it is getting smaller, it is called a waning Moon.

THINGS TO DO

Every night for one month, look at the Moon. Make one drawing of the Moon's shape each night. Label your sketch with the date, time, and what phase you think it is.

Saturday
March 23
9:20pm

Crescent
Moon

The Moon's surface

You can explore the Moon's craters, highlands, and seas. Different features are visible as the Moon changes phase.

SPOTTING CRATERS

Look for craters when the Moon is fuller than a half circle. They were made when meteors or asteroids hit the surface.

ARISTARCHUS

On the upper left of the Moon, this crater is one of the brightest spots you can see. It is 450 million years old.

COPERNICUS

Below and to the right of Aristarchus, this crater is about one mile deep. It is named after the Polish astronomer Nicolaus Copernicus.

TYCHO

This crater is toward the bottom of the Moon. It is 53 miles across. The bright rays coming out from it were made when a giant meteor struck the Moon.

THE MOON'S SEAS

The dark patches on the Moon are called seas, but they don't hold any water. Instead, they are smooth, rocky plains, made when molten rock flooded parts of the Moon's surface long ago.

LOOK FOR THE TERMINATOR

The **terminator** is the dividing line between the sunlit part of the Moon and the part that is in darkness.

Terminator ▶

Exploring the Moon

The Moon is the only place in our solar system—apart from Earth—where people have walked. Six crewed spacecraft and many more robot probes have landed on the Moon. They sent back lots of information and even collected rock samples from the surface.

LOOKING FOR APOLLO

Using a pair of binoculars, try to find the places where the six Apollo spacecraft landed on the Moon. Use the picture of the Moon here to help you. The locations of the Moon's craters and dark seas make great pointers.

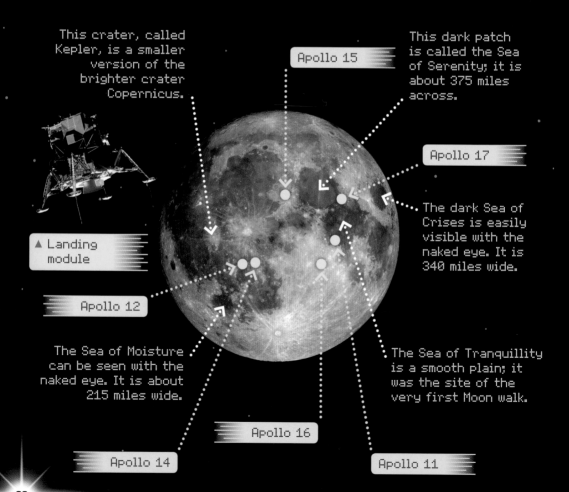

This crater, called Kepler, is a smaller version of the brighter crater Copernicus.

Apollo 15

This dark patch is called the Sea of Serenity; it is about 375 miles across.

Apollo 17

The dark Sea of Crises is easily visible with the naked eye. It is 340 miles wide.

▲ Landing module

Apollo 12

The Sea of Moisture can be seen with the naked eye. It is about 215 miles wide.

The Sea of Tranquillity is a smooth plain; it was the site of the very first Moon walk.

Apollo 16

Apollo 14

Apollo 11

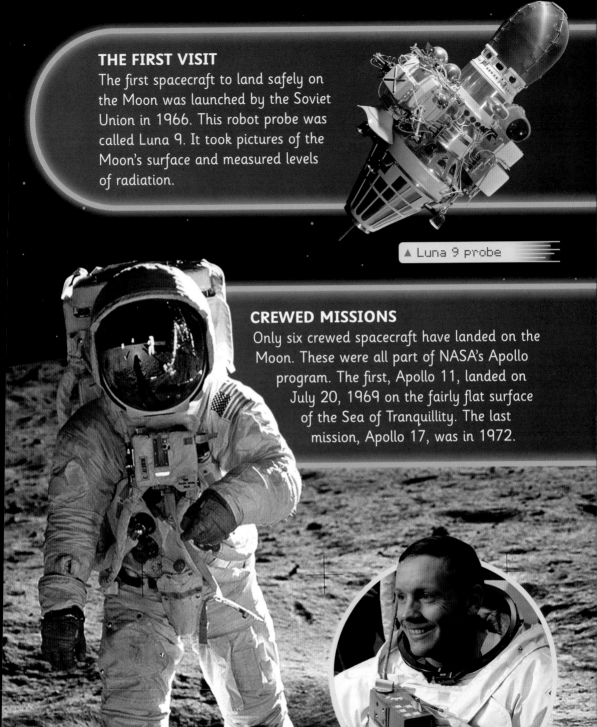

THE FIRST VISIT

The first spacecraft to land safely on the Moon was launched by the Soviet Union in 1966. This robot probe was called Luna 9. It took pictures of the Moon's surface and measured levels of radiation.

▲ Luna 9 probe

CREWED MISSIONS

Only six crewed spacecraft have landed on the Moon. These were all part of NASA's Apollo program. The first, Apollo 11, landed on July 20, 1969 on the fairly flat surface of the Sea of Tranquillity. The last mission, Apollo 17, was in 1972.

▲ **Astronaut** Neil Armstrong was the first person to walk on the Moon.

Lunar eclipses

A lunar eclipse is a rare but beautiful sight in the night sky. It happens when the Moon passes through the shadow cast by Earth. For this to occur, the full Moon and Sun must be exactly on opposite sides of Earth. This does not happen often, and so lunar eclipses can only be seen on Earth about twice a year.

WATCHING LUNAR ECLIPSES

You can enjoy watching a total lunar eclipse with unaided eyes or binoculars. A lunar eclipse takes several hours from start to finish, with the Moon completely covered by Earth's shadow for about one hour. Since the eclipse occurs slowly, a good way to watch it is to look at the Moon every 20 minutes and keep track of how the shadowed part of the Moon is changing.

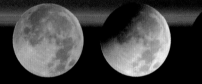

The shadow of Earth ▲ passes over the Moon during an eclipse.

HOW ECLIPSES HAPPEN

Earth's shadow passes slowly over the Moon during an eclipse. Sometimes the Moon is completely shadowed by Earth; this is called a total eclipse. Sometimes the Moon only passes through the edge of Earth's shadow; this is called a partial eclipse.

Sun ▶

TURNING RED!

When the Moon goes into the shadow of Earth during a total eclipse, it turns an orange color. This is because light from the Sun bends slightly as it passes through Earth's atmosphere. Dust in the atmosphere turns the light orange before it strikes the Moon.

MAKE A DATE

Total lunar eclipses will occur on these dates in these places:

- October 8, 2014: Australia, South America
- April 4, 2015: Asia, Australia, South America
- July 27, 2018: Europe, Africa, Asia, Australia
- January 21, 2019: Europe, Africa, South America

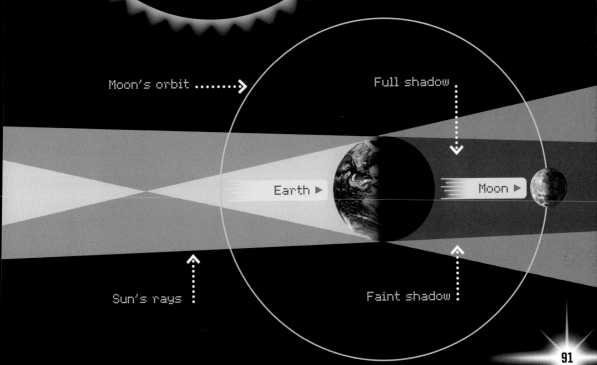

Moon's orbit ········>

Full shadow

Earth ▶

Moon ▶

Sun's rays

Faint shadow

Solar eclipses are awesome sights. See how they happen and find out when the next one is due, and how to watch it safely.

Meteor showers can light up the sky—but where and when can you see them?

What is a comet and when can you expect to see one? Learn more about these spectacular balls of dirty ice.

Unusual Sights

Discover how the solar wind causes our atmosphere to light up.

Find out the difference between a meteor and a meteorite.

Meteors

Meteors are nature's fireworks. These fast-moving streaks of light in the night sky are sometimes called "shooting stars," but they having nothing at all to do with stars. Rather, they are small rocky objects or particles from space that burn up when they enter Earth's atmosphere.

METEOR SHOWERS

You can see meteors at any time of the year, but some months are especially good for seeing lots of these "shooting stars." Meteor showers can be spectacular, with hundreds of meteors visible in an hour, all seeming to come from one part of the night sky.

GETTING PREPARED

You don't need any equipment to watch meteor showers—just your eyes! For the best chance of seeing a meteor shower, check when a shower is due, and look in the area of its constellation. If possible, choose a dark, moonless night and move well away from streetlights.

Lie back on the ground or on a ▲ deck chair and watch the show.

Earth

Comet

Comet dust

BURNING COMET DUST

Comets that pass close to Earth leave behind huge amounts of tiny dust particles. Meteor showers occur when Earth—in its orbit around the Sun—passes through those leftover bits of comet dust. When this happens, lots of dust grains crash into Earth's atmosphere and burn up to make a meteor shower.

Did you know?

A meteor is a particle—from a dust grain to a small rock in size—that burns up in Earth's atmosphere. If it does not completely burn up and crashes to the ground, it is then known as a **meteorite**.

◄ Meteorite

Meteor streaks ▲

▲ Look for the
shape of Perseus
in the sky.

▲ Meteor streaks

The Perseid shower

The Perseid meteor shower happens every year between July and August. At the peak of the shower in mid-August, there can be between 50 and 75 streaks every hour. However, if you are watching from the Southern Hemisphere, you might only see about 10 to 20 meteors per hour.

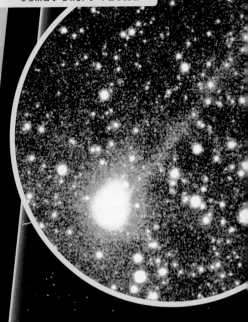

ASTROFACTS

>> The dust that makes the Perseid meteor shower was left behind by a comet called Swift-Tuttle.

>> Comet Swift-Tuttle was last seen in our skies in 1992 and won't appear again until 2126.

>> The meteors that burn up in Earth's atmosphere move at nearly 134,000 miles per hour.

SPOTTING THE PERSEIDS

The Perseid shower appears to spread out from the constellation of Perseus. Look up at that area of the sky, and at patches of dark sky around this constellation.

▲ If you like camping, why not plan a trip during the dates of the meteor showers?

The Leonid shower

The Leonid meteor shower is special because it can turn into a meteor storm. In 1966, night sky watchers in the United States saw nearly 3,000 meteors every minute! But these big storms are rare, and in most years you will see about 10 to 20 meteors every hour.

SPOTTING THE LEONIDS

The best time of the year to look for the Leonid meteors is from mid- to late November. The shower is clearer after midnight, and it helps if it's a moonless night. The meteors appear in all parts of the sky, but if you trace them back, you'll see that they spread out from the constellation of Leo. The Leonids can be seen from both hemispheres.

METEOR STORM

People watching the Leonids in 1833 said they could see 100,000 meteors in the sky every hour. Some made drawings of this amazing sight. The next big Leonid storm is due in 2023, when Earth will pass through a thick cloud of comet dust.

The Leonid meteor ▲ shower of 1833.

▼ From 2014 to 2020, look for the Leonids on the nights of November 16, 17, and 18.

ASTROFACTS

>> The Leonid meteor shower is caused by Earth passing through the dust left behind by a comet called Tempel-Tuttle.

>> The light streaks you see are particles burning up in Earth's atmosphere with temperatures as high as 3,000 degrees Fahrenheit. Most are no bigger than peas.

The Geminid shower

The Geminid meteor shower is one of the best of the year. You can see it from both hemispheres, over all parts of the world. This shower gets its name from the constellation of Gemini, because the meteors seem to spread out from that part of the sky.

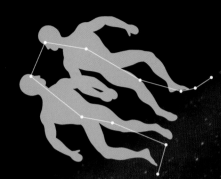

▼ Look for the constellation of Gemini ("The Twins").

FIREBALLS

In the Southern Hemisphere, the constellation of Gemini is always close to the horizon, so you're likely to see fewer meteors than in the Northern Hemisphere. If you get lucky, the Geminids can produce a few very bright "fireballs" that really light up the night sky!

SPOTTING THE GEMINIDS

You can see the Geminid meteor shower every year during the first three weeks of December. It's at its most spectacular around December 14–15. The best time to look is from 9pm onward when you may see up to 120 meteor flashes every hour.

THINGS TO DO

After you've watched a meteor shower, try drawing what you saw. Take a large piece of black paper and use white, yellow, and orange chalk to draw the streaks of light in the sky. Show the horizon and any tall trees and buildings too. Try to add in the constellation from which the meteors seemed to spread out.

▲ A Geminid meteor fireball.

Dancing lights in the sky

Sometimes the night sky shimmers with a beautiful display of glowing lights called **aurorae**. You can usually see aurorae only in countries that are close to Earth's North or South poles, such as Iceland, Norway, Canada, Southern Australia, and New Zealand.

SPOTTING AURORAE

Watching aurorae is simple, but you need a clear, dark night and lots of electrical activity in the atmosphere. Try to find a spot in the country, away from city lights. Around midnight, let your eyes get used to the dark, then face north (or south if you are in the Southern Hemisphere) and look close to the horizon. The aurorae mostly appear as faint green or reddish glows.

WHAT ARE AURORAE?

Aurorae happen because super-hot gases are thrown off by the Sun. These gases include electrified particles. When the particles reach Earth's magnetic field, they get dragged into Earth's atmosphere near the North and South poles. They smash into **atoms** in the atmosphere, making glowing halos of light.

Aurorae are named after the Roman goddess of dawn, Aurora, who brought the light of day in her chariot. In the Northern Hemisphere these dancing light shows are called the *aurora borealis*, or Northern Lights. In the Southern Hemisphere, they are called the *aurora australis*, or Southern Lights.

Roman goddess ▲
Aurora

ASTROFACTS

>> Most aurorae occur about 60 miles up in the atmosphere.

>> The particles thrown out by the Sun take at least two days to travel the 93 million miles to Earth.

>> Aurorae can be green, yellow, orange, or red and look like rippling sheets of light.

International ▲
Space Station

Fleeting satellites

Right now, there are around 2,500 artificial satellites and spacecraft orbiting Earth. Many of the satellites can be seen in the night sky because, like the planets and the Moon, they reflect sunlight.

EYES IN THE SKY

Satellites are vital to modern life. They send telephone and television signals around the world, help predict the weather, and gather important information about our planet and the universe beyond. To stay in orbit, satellites zoom around Earth at nearly 19,000 miles per hour, and complete a lap around the planet in just two hours.

SPOTTING SATELLITES

On a dark night you can spot more than 20 satellites passing across the sky every hour. You'll need to have a good view over a wide region of the night sky. Unlike meteors, which streak by in a flash, a satellite will appear as a starlike speck of light that lingers for five minutes or more as it travels from one horizon to the other. Most satellites travel from west to east.

INTERNATIONAL SPACE STATION

The International Space Station (ISS) is the largest object we have ever built in space. It is about the size of a football field. The ISS orbits about 220 miles above Earth and sometimes appears brighter than Venus! The ISS can be seen just before sunrise or after sunset, crossing the sky from the west. It might look like a fast-moving airplane, but the ISS does not have any flashing lights.

The International Space ▲ Station passes overhead at 17,000 miles per hour.

ASTROFACTS

>> Most satellites orbit about 250 miles above our planet.

>> The first human-made object orbited Earth in 1957. It was a basketball-sized satellite called Sputnik 1.

Sputnik 1 ▲

Solar eclipses

A solar eclipse may be the greatest show in the sky. It happens when the Moon passes directly between the Sun and Earth. The Moon then blocks out most of the Sun's light. A total eclipse of the Sun only happens about once every two years.

HOW ECLIPSES HAPPEN

Solar eclipses are rare because the Sun, Moon, and Earth have to be in exactly the right places in space. And you have to be standing in the right place on Earth, at the right time, to see it! Sometimes the Moon only covers a part of the Sun, allowing some sunlight to get through. This is called a partial eclipse.

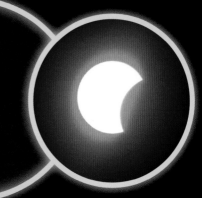

▲ Partial eclipse

BITING THE SUN

When an eclipse starts, you'll see the Moon move slowly across the Sun. It looks like the Moon has taken a bite out of the Sun! Slowly, over the next few hours, the "bite" will get larger and larger. Finally, the Moon will fully cover the Sun. This moment is called **totality**, and lasts only a few minutes. The light of day turns into dark night! You might notice a few stars, birds will stop singing, and it may feel slightly cooler.

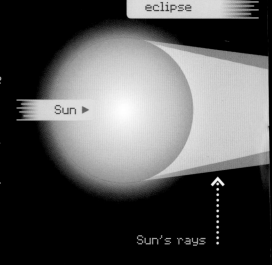

Sun ▶

Sun's rays

The stages of ▶ an eclipse

DANGER! WARNING!

You must NEVER look directly at the Sun with your eyes, or through binoculars or a telescope. Looking at the Sun is very dangerous and can cause blindness. To find out how to watch an eclipse safely, turn to the next page.

turn to the next page.

ASTROFACTS

>> During a solar eclipse, the Moon's shadow moves across the surface of Earth at more than 900 miles per hour.

>> Total solar eclipses happen about once every 1.5 years.

>> There are at least two partial eclipses per year somewhere on Earth.

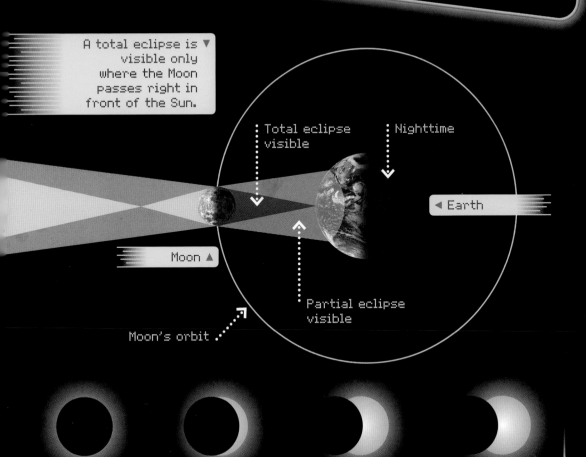

A total eclipse is ▼ visible only where the Moon passes right in front of the Sun.

Total eclipse visible

Nighttime

◄ Earth

Moon ▲

Partial eclipse visible

Moon's orbit

Watching eclipses safely

To watch a solar eclipse, get the help of an adult. You can't look directly at the Sun so you'll need to project its image onto a screen by making a simple pinhole viewer (see right).

WATCHING THROUGH GLASSES

You can buy special eclipse glasses that safely filter most of the Sun's rays. Wearing these glasses can let you watch a solar eclipse safely for a few minutes. Ask an adult to buy a pair of these glasses— they are NOT the same as sunglasses!

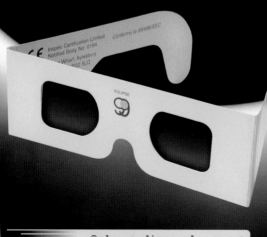

Inspec Certification Limited
Notified Body No: 0194
Wharf, Aylesbury
2 5LO

Conforms to 89/686-EEC

CE

ECLIPSE

Solar eclipse glasses ▲

In a total eclipse, ▲ you may see the ghostly white light of the Sun's outermost region, called the corona, as it shimmers around the Moon.

THINGS TO DO

1 To make a pinhole viewer, you'll need two pieces of stiff cardboard or posterboard, one of which must be white because it will be your screen. Cut a small square in one piece, and then tape a piece of aluminum foil over the square.

2 Next, make a pinhole in the middle of the foil.

3 Place the white screen piece on the ground or against a chair. With the Sun behind you, hold up the cardboard with the pinhole and line it up so that the Sun's image falls on the screen. You'll have to move the pinhole part up and down to get a large, clear image of the Sun on the white surface.

MAKE A DATE

Total solar eclipses will be visible on these dates at these places:

- March 20, 2015: parts of Iceland, Europe, North America, and Asia
- March 9, 2016: East Asia and Australia
- August 21, 2017: parts of North and South America
- July 2, 2019: South America
- December 14, 2020: South America

Bright comets often ▶
show two flowing tails,
making a "V" shape. One
of the tails is blue and
made of gas. The other
is creamy yellow and
made of dust.

Great comets

A bright comet with a huge tail sweeping across the night sky is one of nature's most amazing sights. Comets don't appear often, but when they do, be prepared and make the most of it. Some comets only get close enough to be seen once every 200 years!

WHAT ARE COMETS?

Comets are big dusty snowballs that travel around the Sun in very long, stretched-out orbits. They are icy leftovers from the time that the Sun and solar system formed about 4.5 billion years ago. The icy part of a comet, called its nucleus, is quite small—few are much more than 10 miles (15 kilometers) across.

▲ The nucleus of
the comet called
Tempel 1.

THE TAIL OF A COMET

Most of the time, comets are so far from the Sun that we can't see them. But when the long orbit of a comet brings it close to the Sun, something special happens. The heat of the Sun warms the ice of the comet's nucleus and boils it off. The boiled ice and dust forms tails that stream millions of miles behind the comet, always pointing away from the Sun. We can then see the comet as a glowing head with a long tail.

THE PATH OF A COMET

A comet's elongated orbit brings it close to the Sun. This is when the comet becomes visible.

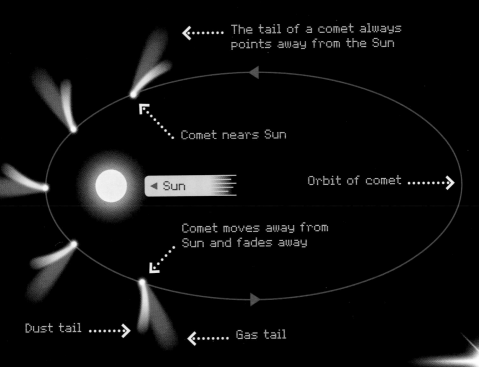

The tail of a comet always points away from the Sun

Comet nears Sun

Sun

Orbit of comet ....>

Comet moves away from Sun and fades away

Dust tail ....>

<....... Gas tail

ASTROFACTS

>> Halley's comet is one of the best-known comets. It last appeared in our skies in 1986, and won't return again until 2061.

>> In July 1994 a comet called Shoemaker-Levy 9 broke apart and smashed into the giant planet Jupiter.

>> Some comets crash into the Sun and vanish.

Spotting comets

Some comets appear in our skies regularly every few hundred years. But others are less predictable. Even astronomers can't be sure when the next great comet will come. The biggest comets can easily be seen even from brightly lit towns and cities.

GREAT COMETS OF THE PAST

There have been some amazing comets in history. The great comet of 1744 was so bright that it be could be seen in the morning sky. Comet Ikeya-Seki was the brightest of the 20th century. In October 1965, it was nearly ten times brighter than the full Moon!

▲ This painting shows Donati's comet over London in 1858.

Did you know?

Comets are such an awesome sight in the sky that people in the past thought they were messages from the gods. Because some comets looked like swords in the sky, some people took them to be signs of war and disaster to come.

WHERE TO LOOK

When a comet appears, it doesn't move across the sky in a flash, like a meteor. Because comets are very far away, they stay in the sky from night to night, for weeks. Most comets are faint and you'll need binoculars to see them. Even then, you may only see the tail. You'll need to check astronomy websites to find out where to look.

Glossary

ASTEROID
A large rocky object in the solar system. Most asteroids orbit the Sun in a belt between Mars and Jupiter.

ASTRONAUT
A person who travels in space.

ASTRONOMER
A scientist who studies objects in space, such as planets and stars.

ATMOSPHERE
Layers of gases that surround a planet, moon, or star.

ATOM
A minuscule building block that makes up all matter.

AURORAE
Light displays caused by particles from the Sun that enter the Earth's (or other planet's) atmosphere around the north or south poles.

BILLION
The number equal to 1,000 million. It is written as 1 followed by 9 zeros.

BLACK HOLE
A region of space around a very small and extremely massive object within which the gravity is so strong that not even light can escape.

CARBON DIOXIDE
A gas given off by animals and taken in by plants. It is present in the atmospheres of several planets.

COMET
A small icy object, made of gas and dust, that orbits around the Sun.

CONSTELLATION
An imaginary pattern or shape drawn in the sky by connecting lines between different stars.

DAY
The length of time it takes Earth (or any planet) to spin once on its axis.

DIAMETER
The length of a straight line passing through the center of a circle and connecting two points on the circumference (the edge of the circle).

DUST (IN SPACE)
Tiny solid particles that float in the space between stars.

ECLIPSE

The event that occurs when one body in space passes in front of another and blocks out the light from the more distant of the two objects.

ELEMENT

A pure chemical, such as hydrogen, oxygen, carbon, iron, and so on.

EQUATOR (EARTH'S)

The line around the Earth that is the boundary between the Northern and Southern hemispheres.

GALAXY

A collection of billions of stars, gas, and dust held together by gravity.

GRAVITY

A force that pulls two objects together. It depends on the amount of matter in the objects and their distance apart.

HELIUM

The second-lightest and second most common element in the universe. The product of the nuclear fusion of hydrogen in stars.

HEMISPHERE

The half of Earth (or another planet) between the North Pole or South Pole and the equator.

HORIZON

The line where the ground and sky appear to meet.

HYDROGEN

The lightest and most common element in the universe.

LATITUDE

The location of a point on Earth relative to the equator. There are ninety degrees of latitude north and south of the line of the equator.

LIGHT-YEAR

The distance traveled by light in space in one year. This is a distance of about 5,900,000,000,000 miles (9,500,000,000,000 kilometers).

METEOR

A bright streak of light in the sky caused when a small rocky object enters Earth's atmosphere and burns up.

METEORITE
The remains of a rocky and metallic object that plunges from space and lands on Earth's surface.

MILKY WAY
A spiral galaxy that contains over 100 billion stars, including the Sun and its solar system.

MILLION
The number 1,000,000, written as 1 followed by 6 zeros.

MOON
A small rocky body that moves around a planet.

NEBULA
A cloud of gas and dust in space. New stars may be made in a nebula.

NUCLEAR FUSION
A process in which lighter elements are joined together to make a heavier element; enormous amounts of energy are released in the process.

ORBIT
The path taken by an object as it moves around another body. The Moon follows an orbit around Earth.

PHASE
The changing sunlit part of the Moon or inner planet—as seen from Earth— as it travels in its orbit around Earth or the Sun.

PLANET
A large object, made up mostly of rock or gas, that orbits a star.

PLANISPHERE
A movable, circular map of the stars in the sky that can be used to show the appearance of the night sky at any given time and date.

POLES (NORTH AND SOUTH)
The two points on a planet's surface that are farthest away from its equator.

SATELLITE
Any object (natural or human-made) that orbits another body in space.

SOLAR SYSTEM
The group of eight planets, many dwarf planets, and other objects orbiting the Sun.

SPACECRAFT
A vehicle for travel beyond Earth's atmosphere.

SPIRAL (GALAXY)
A galaxy with long arms that wind into a bulge at the center. It is the most common type of galaxy.

STAR
A huge ball of hot gas that gives out energy from the process of nuclear fusion. Part of this energy is released as visible light.

STAR CLUSTER
A collection of hundreds or thousands of stars formed together.

SUPERGIANT
A star that has swollen in size to tens or even hundreds of times larger than the Sun is today.

SUPERNOVA
A violent event that occurs when a massive star explodes.

TELESCOPE
A device that uses lenses or mirrors to magnify the view of distant objects.

TEMPERATURE
A measure of the amount of heat energy in a substance.

TERMINATOR
The line that divides the night (shadowed portion) and day (sunlit portion) of the Moon.

TOTALITY
The path on Earth's surface along which a total solar eclipse is visible.

TRILLION
The number equal to a million million. It is written as 1 followed by 12 zeros.

UNIVERSE
The huge space that contains all of time, matter, and energy. .

VOLCANO
An opening in a planet's surface through which hot liquid rock is thrown up.

YEAR
The length of time it takes a planet to orbit the Sun.

Index